## DATE DUE

| | |
|---|---|
| NOV 1 0 2010 | |
| JUN 0 8 2011 | |
| JUL 1 9 2011 | |
| MAR 3 1 2012 | |
| | |
| | |
| | |
| | |
| | |
| | |
| | |
| | |
| | |
| | |
| | |
| | |
| | |

# SPORTS FOR SPROUTS

# PLAYGROUND GAMES

Tracy Nelson Maurer

ROURKE PUBLISHING

www.rourkepublishing.com

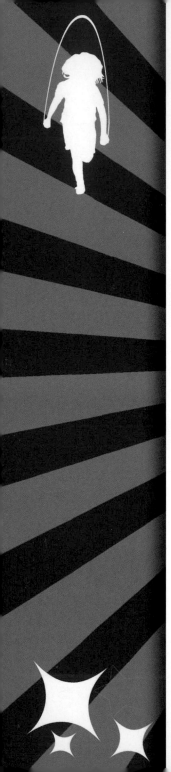

www.rourkepublishing.com

Photo credits: All photos © Blue Door Publishing except cover: © Juriah Mosin

Editor: Jeanne Sturm

Cover and page design by Nicola Stratford, bdpublishing.com


Library of Congress Cataloging-in-Publication Data

Maurer, Tracy, 1965-
 Playground games : sports for sprouts / Tracy Nelson Maurer.
     p. cm.
 Includes bibliographical references and index.
 ISBN 978-1-61590-233-0 (Hard cover) (alk. paper)
 ISBN 978-1-61590-473-0 (Soft cover)
 1. Playgrounds--Juvenile literature. 2.  Games--Juvenile literature.  I. Title.
 GV423.M395 2011
 796--dc22
                                        2009047303


Rourke Publishing
Printed in the United States of America, North Mankato, Minnesota
033010
033010LP

www.rourkepublishing.com - rourke@rourkepublishing.com
Post Office Box 643328 Vero Beach, Florida 32964

We slide, swing, and play games at the **playground**.

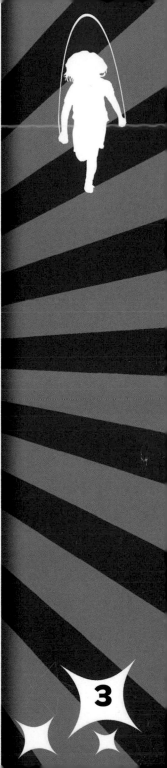

We play **tag**.

5

We play **hopscotch.**

Two feet! One foot!
She hops to her bag.

9

We play **kickball**.

11

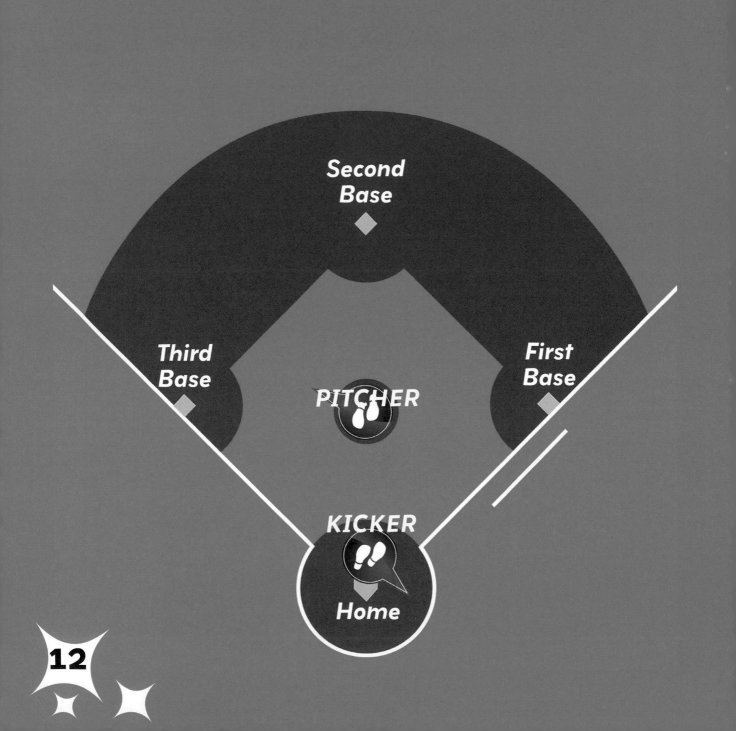

Second
Base

Third
Base

First
Base

PITCHER

KICKER

Home

12

The pitcher rolls the ball to the kicker.

The kicker runs the **bases.**

We skip rope to silly **chants.**

One potato, two potatoes, three potatoes, four.

Digga-digga-dig! Now count some more.

Keep counting until the jumper misses!

We take turns and follow the rules.

We have fun!

21

# Picture Glossary

**bases** (BAYSS-ez): There are four bases on a kickball field. The kicker must touch them all for his or her team to earn a point.

**chants** (CHANTS): Jump-ropers say chants in rhymes or silly phrases to keep time or challenge the jumper.

**hopscotch** (HOP-skoch): Players toss a marker onto numbers drawn in chalk or painted on a sidewalk. Players hop to the next number with every turn.

**kickball** (KIK-bawl): Kickball has rules much like baseball. Players kick a rolled ball and run to touch each base from first to home.

**playground** (PLAY-ground): A playground is a park or safe area for running that may also have play equipment.

**tag** (TAG): In tag, one player tries to tap another player; the tagged player then becomes *it* — the chaser.

**23**

## Index

## Websites

www.pecentral.org/websites/kidsites.html

www.learn4good.com/kids/sports.htm

www.sikids.com

## About the Author

Tracy Nelson Maurer loves to play with her two children and husband in their neighborhood near Minneapolis, Minnesota. She holds an MFA in Writing for Children & Young Adults from Hamline University, and has written more than 70 books for young readers.